Nursery Education
in Converted Space

Department of Education and Science

Building Bulletin 56

Building Bulletin 56: Nursery Education in Converted Space

Due to an industrial dispute at Her Majesty's Stationery Office, this publication
is not available for sale at HMSO or other bookshops at present. The Department
of Education and Science is also unable to supply any further copies.

October 1978

Acknowledgements

The Design Team would like to acknowledge the assistance received from the Nottinghamshire Education Authority, the Nottingham County Architects Department, and many others who helped with the study. In particular they would like to record their appreciation of the contribution of Mr John Plumb (Senior Assistant Director of Education), Mrs Margaret Cornish (Nursery Adviser) and other colleagues in the Education Department, and the Head Teachers and Staffs of the schools involved in the project.

The Design Team:

Dick Thompson, Dick Post, Paul Tanner, Liz Frazer, Jane Sachs (Architects).
Mike Lawton (Quantity Surveyor).
George Bailey (M + E Engineer).
Herbert Story (HMI).
Bridget Sanders and Andy Thompson (Graduate Trainee Architects) helped with supervision of the building contract.
The main Contractors for the work were:
J. M. Richards & Co. (Mansfield) Ltd.
Drawings of the four nurseries by Gavin Rowe appear on the following pages:

Glenbrook	26, 35, 37
Robert Jones Infant and Junior Schools	7, 8, 31
Carlton Netherfield	3, 4
Clifton Whitegate	12, 15, 20

Contents

Bibliography

DESIGN NOTE 1: Building for Nursery Education (DES: 1968).

DESIGN NOTE 11: Chaucer Infant and Nursery School, Ilkeston, Derbyshire (DES: 1973).

BUILDING BULLETIN 38: School Furniture Dimensions: Standing and Reaching (HMSO: 1967: price 65p).

Standards for School Premises Regulations 1972 (SI 2051: HMSO: price 13½p).

Guidelines for Environmental Design and Energy Conservation in Educational Buildings (DES: revised version to be published in 1978).

A Right to be Children; Designing for the Education of the Under-fives (1976: RIBA Publications Limited: price £3.00).

Introduction

1. The value of the contribution which nursery education can make to the educational and social development of young children, especially those from disadvantaged backgrounds, is now widely acknowledged. Since the expansion of nursery education began with the Urban Programme in 1969 over 50,000 new nursery places have been brought into use in England and Wales. Over the next few years resources for further expansion will be very scarce and it will therefore be especially important to ensure that such resources as are available are used to the fullest advantage.

2. Guidance on designing for nursery education was given in the Department's Design Note 1: Building for Nursery Education in 1968[1]. This was followed in 1973 by Design Note 11 on the Chaucer Infant and Nursery School at Ilkeston. Both were concerned with the design of new buildings[2]. The decline in primary age population in many areas of the country will release space in existing schools which, if suitably adapted, might provide accommodation for nursery use at a cost significantly less than that of a new building. This bulletin describes projects for adapting surplus space in four Nottinghamshire primary schools of different types and vintages which were carried out between 1974 and 1976 as a development project by the Architects and Building Branch of the Department of Education and Science.

---

[1] The statutory minimum requirements for Nursery Schools and Nursery Classes are set out in Part IV of the Standards for School Premises Regulations 1972.

[2] A list of all the publications referred to in the text can be found on pages 47 & 48.

1

The Educational Background

3. During the first five years of life children develop in physical size and control and in the ability to communicate faster than at any other time. Young children learn a great deal through exploration and experiment, through making and modelling, through imaginative role playing and through acting out the adult activities that they observe. Nursery education, if it is to be effective, must provide opportunities for children to engage in these activities in company with other children at about the same stage of development under the supervision of skilled and experienced adults who can stimulate and guide their development.

4. If the nursery is to bring the maximum benefit to the children it should be complementary to the home. It will only succeed fully if the parents are taken into partnership and know what the nursery is doing and why. For this reason nurseries welcome visits by parents and encourage them to stay with their children and meet the staff. Moreover the nursery can be a natural focus for many others in the community concerned with the care of the under fives. During the investigation stage of the project the team saw several examples of close cooperation with community teachers, social workers and health visitors. Before moving to a detailed account of the project it may be useful to describe briefly the forms of nursery provision available for the under five age group.

Nursery Schools and Units

5. Nursery Schools and Nursery Units (classes attached to primary schools) cater for children from three years old until they reach statutory school age. With the exception of a small number of private nursery schools, they are maintained by the local education authority.

6. Nursery Units or Classes are dependent for many facilities on the infant or primary schools to which they are attached. Nursery schools on the other hand are separate organisations with their own head teachers and are largely self sufficient. It is expected that the majority of pupils attending nurseries will do so part-time—usually for a single three hour session in the morning or afternoon. However a small number may, for a variety of reasons, need to attend for a full day. Nurseries vary in size from a twenty place nursery class to a nursery school or unit of up to sixty places (and occasionally more). A staffing ratio of around one adult to thirteen children is usual. Usually a third to a half of the staff are qualified teachers who are supported by qualified nursery nurses.

7. In a few cases nursery schools have been organised so as to provide an extended day. One such nursery which the team visited operated from 8 am to 6 pm for forty-nine weeks of the year. Only a small minority of children attended for the whole day—most were part-timers—but it was possible to vary the timing and length of attendance to suit particular needs. This extended day arrangement offers a more intensive use of accommodation than the conventionally organised nursery school or class.

8. Although there are a few special nursery schools which cater for severely handicapped children, it is generally accepted that children with moderate handicaps may be accommodated in ordinary nursery schools, which must be designed to allow for this. The number of handicapped children admitted to any one nursery is limited by the need to preserve a balance so

Carlton Netherfield

that normal children are not outnumbered or adversely affected.

Play Groups
9. There are many different kinds of play groups but all must be registered with the Social Services Department of the local authority. Most are members of the Pre-School Play Group Association. The premises which they use must be approved by the Social Services Department and some are assisted by grants, loans of equipment and local authority expertise. Children normally attend for a half-day session, in the morning or afternoon, or between one and five days a week. The groups are staffed by volunteers, usually parents, of whom one is generally qualified as a play group leader.

Day Nurseries
10. These are run by the Social Services Department of the local authority and accept children from a few months up to five years old. They provide all-day care from around 8 am to 6 pm. The organisation is generally on the basis of small "family" groups, each supervised by an adult. Day nurseries are staffed by a matron with either child care or nursery experience, assisted by trained nursery nurses.

Pre-School Centres
11. A small number of these centres have recently been established in new purpose-built accommodation. They combine the facilities of a day nursery with those of a nursery school and cater for children from a few months up to five years old. They are run and staffed jointly by the Social Services and Education Departments of the local authority and have both a head teacher and matron. In one centre visited by the team the day care section of the centre was open from 8 am to 5.30 pm whilst the nursery school was open from 9 am to 5.30 pm. This centre contained a twenty place day nursery and a sixty place nursery school.

3

Carlton Netherfield

Purpose of the Project

12. Early in 1974 a small team from the Development Group within Architects and Building Branch visited a number of local education authorities to discuss informally general policy on nursery provision and in particular the practicability of converting surplus primary accommodation for nursery use. One of these discussions prompted the Director of Education for Nottinghamshire to invite the Development Group to collaborate in a project involving a number of the authority's primary schools.

13. The main objectives of the project were as follows:

    i. to demonstrate that the principles of nursery design which had been developed for new buildings could be successfully applied in the adaptation of surplus accommodation in a variety of existing buildings;

    ii. to integrate the nurseries into the existing schools so as not to affect adversely the provision for other age groups and to prepare a development plan for the school as a whole;

    iii. to landscape the existing spaces for nursery use and to provide easy access to them from the nurseries;

    iv. to provide facilities for parents and other adults which would encourage them to participate in the work of the nurseries;

    v. to investigate other facilities for the under fives in the areas served by the schools and to plan the projects so that they might provide a focus for those working with this age group;

    vi. to provide information on the costs of conversion and to compare the value for money of a conversion with that of a new building.

14. Four primary schools were provisionally selected for the introduction of nursery units:

The Carlton Netherfield Infant School, built in 1893 and 1903 at Netherfield on the outskirts of Nottingham and serving an area of mainly Victorian terraced housing (40 place unit);

The Robert Jones Infant and Junior Schools, built in the 1930s in the mining village of Blidworth in Nottinghamshire (40 place unit);

Glenbrook Infant School, built in 1949 as part of an extensive campus of several schools at Bilborough, Nottingham's first post war municipal housing estate (40 place unit);

Clifton Whitegate Infant School, Clifton, Nottingham, built in 1954, with an annex added in 1960, on a large municipal housing estate (60 place unit).

The Investigation

Problems and opportunities of conversion

15. During the initial investigatory stage of the project the team visited a number of schools, built mostly before 1900 but some of more recent date, in which nursery accommodation had been successfully provided by adaptation[1]. They also saw examples of imaginative improvisation and self-help by parents and teachers. It was clear that such schools had the advantages of well-established links with the community and of being known and loved, perhaps in retrospect, by the several generations which had attended them. Nursery facilities enabled these schools to extend their educational and social role in the life of the community, particularly where space had been found for a family centre or parents' room.

16. These schools also enjoyed other advantages. The adaptation of surplus accommodation within an existing school offered the opportunity to plan the nursery as an integral part of the school. This in turn encouraged nursery and infant teachers to work more closely together and to overcome some of the problems of differing rates of child development by allowing for the mixing of nursery and infant children whenever this was appropriate. The introduction of the nursery sometimes led to a re-examination of the methods of organisation and teaching used in other parts of the school with beneficial results.

17. In general the space available for nursery use in these schools had become surplus as a result of the fall in the birthrate leading to a decline in the primary school population. However it was apparent that other factors had also played a part. For example, in some areas the decline had been accentuated by rehousing or clearance schemes or by cyclical changes in the population of housing estates where the residents were all very much of an age. Some surplus space was the direct result of a reorganisation of schools in an area leading to changes in the use of accommodation. In other cases the design of a school had provided accommodation which was now unused or under-used—for example, large cloakrooms and toilet areas or excessive circulation spaces.

Selecting the schools

18. In the four Nottinghamshire primary schools provisionally selected for the project it was known

[1]A brief account of the nurseries visited is given at Appendix A.

that some surplus space was available (or would become available) and that each had a good claim on educational and social grounds for nursery facilities. However, the choice needed to be confirmed by a detailed assessment of the schools.

19. Most of the information on the educational, social and economic background of each school came from those who would be directly involved in the nursery developments or whose activities might affect or be affected by them—head teachers and staff, social workers, play group leaders and others. Local play groups and mothers and toddlers groups were seen in action and, in the course of conversations about their work, leaders were told about the proposed nursery developments. Local officers of the social services and leisure services departments came to some of the schools to discuss the possibilities of co-operating over the use of facilities.

Design criteria

20. In the course of assessing the schools a number of general principles were formulated as a basis for design.

Identification of surplus space
21. It was ascertained that surplus space was not required to remedy other serious deficiencies and that adaptation to nursery use would not adversely affect the existing provision for other children and staff.

Future development
22. If the introduction of a nursery is not to jeopardise the future development of the school as a whole a development plan needs to be drawn up. This should be seen not as a detailed blueprint but as a broad strategy for change and improvement which works towards the overall development of the school. The plan may also demonstrate how and where self-help is applicable and provide a framework around which it can be organised. The development plans for Carlton Netherfield, Glenbrook and Blidworth schools are described in detail in paragraphs 79–88.

Quality of accommodation
23. Because a major objective of the project was to demonstrate good nursery design it was important that the accommodation created by conversion should be broadly equivalent in terms of area, variety of facilities, finishes and furniture to that provided in a new building. The requirements for new buildings are

set out in Part IV of The Standards for School Premises Regulations 1972, which are supplemented by guidance in Design Note 1: Building for Nursery Education. They are also covered in the standard nursery brief prepared by the Nottinghamshire authority.

Compensation for deficiencies

24. Where there are serious inherent deficiencies in building or site which cannot be easily remedied some means of compensating for them may be considered. For example, where garden and outside play space is inadequate, as at Carlton Netherfield, some extra indoor space might be provided. This would be a space, different in character from the general nursery spaces, for noisier and larger scale activities. In areas of special social need a more generous allocation of space would allow for a family centre offering more than the usual facilities for parents and small children. Where use outside normal school hours is contemplated minimum areas might be increased to allow for more spaces with a domestic scale and a kitchen which could be used at such times.

Physical condition of building

25. Account needs to be taken of the structural condition of the building in order to avoid heavy investment in a building with only a short life expectancy. The condition and availability of services, though not as critical as the structure, may also be an important factor. In the case of the Nottinghamshire project all the schools were in fairly good structural condition, although services needed to be substantially replaced in three of them.

Robert Jones Infant and
Junior Schools

7

Assessment of the Schools

Robert Jones Infant and Junior Schools, Blidworth

26. Blidworth is a mining village dominated by the colliery where the majority of the men work. The main community facility in the village is the miners welfare club on which the social life of the mining community is centred. At the time of the investigation pre-school provision for children was confined to one flourishing play group, meeting in rather inconvenient accommodation in the village hall, and a mothers and toddlers group which met on one afternoon a week in a local church hall.

27. The school building was of a courtyard pattern common in 1930s, and consisted of classrooms linked by corridors around three sides of a central court, part of which was grassed and planted. The fourth side comprised two small halls, and a large central hall and kitchen shared by the two schools. Cloakroom provision was generous but, although a few internal lavatories had recently been added, the majority remained external. On the outside the building was entirely surrounded by hard paved areas, bounded by roads to north and south and houses on the other two sides. The construction was of load bearing brickwork with a pitched slated roof and the building was in good structural condition.

28. Ceiling heights varied from a maximum of 5.0 m in classrooms and cloakrooms to 2.5 m in corridors and other rooms. The main rooms were lit by tall sash windows with high sills whose proportions emphasised the height of these spaces and were a source of considerable glare. Ceilings and internal walls were finished in painted plaster.

29. During the investigation the infant school roll stood at 235. By 1977 it was expected to decline to 190 and in subsequent years to 140. (In January 1977 the actual number on roll was 161). However before the

Robert Jones Infant and
Junior Schools

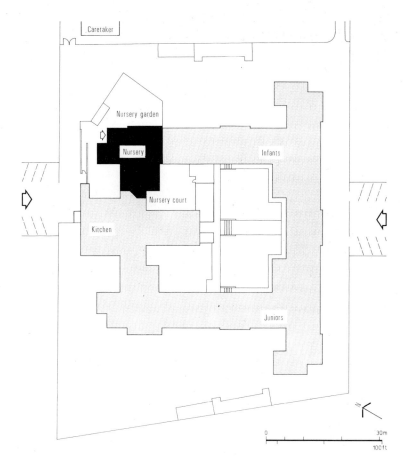

1. Robert Jones Infant and Junior Schools, Blidworth, showing location of nursery unit

space released by the projected decline in numbers could be used it had to be assembled into a single area and some existing uses had to be relocated.

30. After consideration it was decided to locate the proposed forty place nursery in the north-east corner of the building. This placed it in a satisfactory relationship to the infant accommodation and the external spaces without inhibiting the future development of the school as a whole (see figure 1). A small hall and an under-used coat space provided most of the space required in the first phase of the project. The release of a surplus infant classroom at a later stage provided for expansion to include a family centre—in the event both phases were completed at the same time. Certain existing uses within the area (music and movement in the small hall, coats, lavatories and the head teacher's office) were re-accommodated in other parts of the building. This re-accommodation work, although in some ways unwanted, did present the opportunity to take some initial steps in the overall development plan. Details of the development plans for this and other schools are given in paragraphs 79–88.

9

Carlton Netherfield Infant School

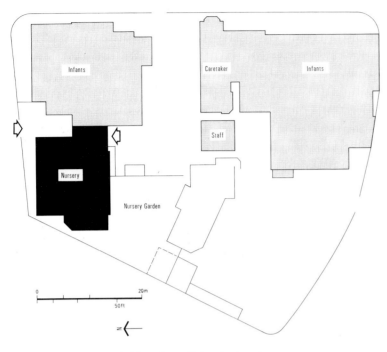

2. Carlton Netherfield Infant School showing
location of nursery unit

31. Netherfield, on the outskirts of Nottingham, was built mainly in the latter half of the last century to house workers in the nearby railway marshalling yards. The area immediately around the school is one of small terraced houses some of which still lack bathrooms and other basic amenities. There is however a strong community feeling in the area and an active Community Association. The considerable community involvement in the school was much encouraged by the head teacher and staff (which included a community teacher) and there was no shortage of parents willing to offer practical help. The mothers ran a drama group which raised funds for the school and the fathers helped to carry out small repair and alteration jobs. Other provision in the area for the under fives consisted of a day nursery run by the Social Services Department and a play group held in a local church hall.

32. The school was built between 1893 and 1903 and is in many ways typical of its period. It consisted of two separate buildings for infants and juniors on a very constricted urban site. Each comprised a series of classrooms clustered around a central hall. There were a number of cloakroom areas, but all pupils' lavatories were outside. The buildings were of load bearing brick with slate roofs and were in good structural condition.

33. External areas were entirely hard and the site was surrounded by high brick walls. While the school had made a brave effort to enliven the site by painting the walls with murals and placing planting boxes on the tarmac the external facilities remained very inadequate. The main entrance doors provided the only access to the outside.

34. The main rooms had a ceiling height of 5.0 m and, as at Blidworth, were lit by very tall windows which accentuated their height. Internal wall finishes were hard and reverberant—mostly painted fair-faced brickwork. Ceilings were plastered. Floors were finished in wood block or vinyl tiles.

35. The surplus space at Carlton was the result not of an immediate decline in infant numbers (although a reduction was expected by 1978–79) but of secondary reorganisation in the area. The transfer of the junior school to the site of a former secondary modern school made both buildings available for the Infant School and nursery. The building originally occupied by the Infant School fell naturally into two sections, one of which could easily be vacated and was of a suitable area to house the proposed forty place nursery (see figure 2). This could be provided with its own entrance and nursery garden whilst maintaining internal links with the rest of the building. The section contained three classrooms, (one of which was divided by a full height timber screen) and a number of smaller rooms.

10

Glenbrook Infants School

36. The school serves part of Nottingham's first post war housing estate at Bilborough. The original population is now ageing and the number of primary age children has declined dramatically. It is too early to know whether this decline will eventually be halted or reversed by an influx of younger families.

37. The majority of the fathers are semi-skilled workers and some mothers work shifts in local factories. The area is fairly well provided with community facilities; there are three community centres on the estate. At the time of the investigation there were two play groups in the area which operated from accommodation in the community centres. A number of neighbouring infant schools also had nursery classes.

38. The school occupies the lower part of a large grassed campus which also includes a junior and a secondary school. It is fairly typical of the immediate post war period—a "finger plan" consisting of two connected spines with enormously extended corridors and teaching space of less than half the gross area of the building. The northern spine contained only ancillary accommodation, mostly lavatories and cloak-rooms which, because of the reduction in class size, were either redundant or under-used. The southern spine consisted of four pairs of classrooms.

39. The northern spine was a single storey pre-cast concrete framed building with brick infill walls, flat concrete roof and concrete floors. Ceiling heights varied from 4.0 m in the main rooms to 2.8 m in the corridors. Although window sills were not as high as those at Blidworth and Carlton, views to the outside were still very limited. These windows were supplemented by high level clerestories and central roof lights.

40. At the time of the investigation the roll of the school had already declined to 165. However it was anticipated that a revision of catchment areas to relieve overcrowding in neighbouring schools would halt this decline and might lead to increased numbers in the future. It was therefore necessary to look for surplus space in the lavish ancillary areas rather than in teaching spaces. The plan form of the building made it peculiarly difficult to adapt and some extension proved to be necessary. In view of this, and the need to provide independent access whilst maintaining contact with the infant school, it was decided to locate the nursery at the western end of the northern spine (see figure 3).

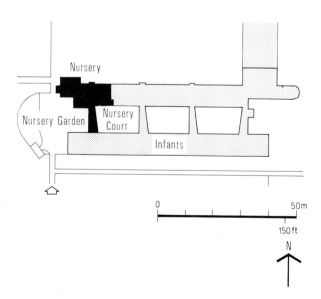

3. Glenbrook Infant School showing location of nursery unit

Clifton Whitegate Infant School

41. The school serves the southern part of the Clifton Estate on the outskirts of Nottingham. This is reputedly one of the largest municipal housing estates in Europe, with a population of 35,000. At the time of the investigation there was one day nursery on the estate and six play groups, although none were very close to the school. The area is not very well provided with community facilities. As at Bilborough the original population is now ageing and the number of primary age children is very much reduced.

42. The school had declined to a point where numbers could easily be accommodated in the main building leaving an annexe built in 1960 on a separate site available for conversion to the proposed sixty place nursery.

43. The annexe was a small prefabricated timber building consisting of three large classrooms and a cloakroom grouped around ancillary rooms (see figure 4). Ceiling heights varied from 3.0 m in the classrooms to 2.5 m in the ancillary rooms. The lavatories were incorporated in the building but entered from the outside. The large windows with low sills provided good visual contact with the outside, but were a source of glare and led to serious overheating in summer. A number of doors provided direct access to the outside.

Clifton Whitegate

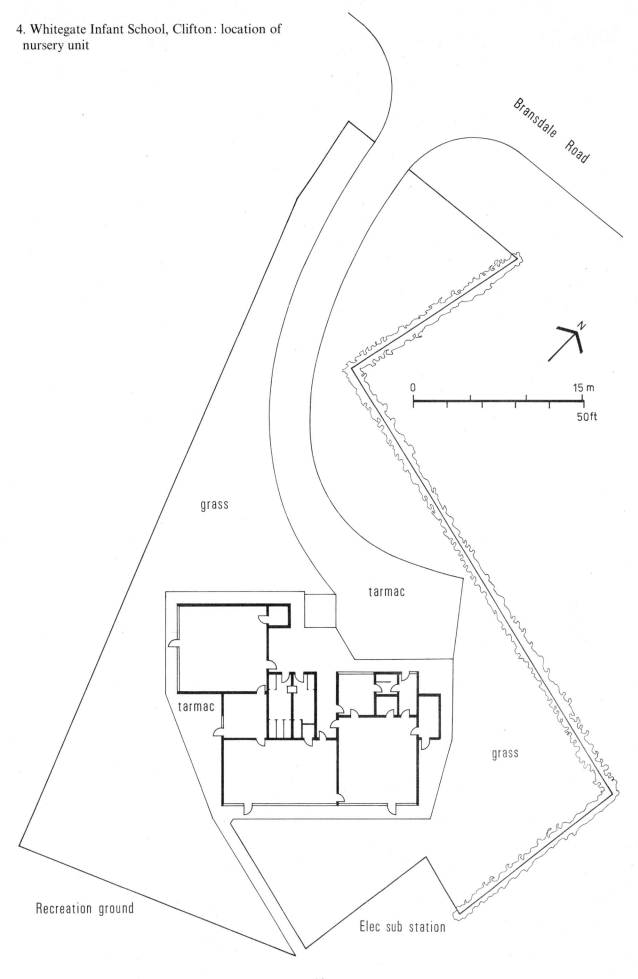

4. Whitegate Infant School, Clifton: location of
   nursery unit

Bransdale Road

15 m

50ft

grass

tarmac

tarmac

grass

Recreation ground

Elec sub station

13

Design of the Projects

44. The standards which a new nursery unit ought to meet are set out in Part IV of the Standards for School Premises Regulations 1972; other desirable features are described in Design Note 1: Building for Nursery Education. These two elements can be summarised together as follows (statutory requirements are given first and marked with an asterisk):

a. Playroom accommodation with a minimum area of 2.3 m² per child*; this should include an activity area and a number of quiet retreats or bays and give access to an outdoor covered play space.

b. An enclosed nursery garden with a minimum area of 9.3 m² per child, of which not less than 3.7 m² should be paved*; storage for outdoor play equipment and toys.

c. Washing and sanitary accommodation; lavatories with a minimum of one WC and one wash basin per ten children and one deep sink per forty children*. These should be easily accessible from the activity area and there should be a utility room with facilities for washing clothes.

d. A separate room which can be used by staff for meeting parents and other visitors and for administrative purposes and can also serve as a quiet room.

e. Storage for teaching materials, equipment and large toys*.

f. Storage for children's outdoor clothing* and other belongings.

g. Facilities for heating drinks where pupils attend part-time and a kitchen for preparing a midday meal for pupils attending full time*. The latter requirement can be satisfied by the kitchen of the attached primary school if it has sufficient capacity.

These elements form the basis for the design of the Nottinghamshire projects. The main ingredients of these designs are described below. They include certain items such as a family centre which, though important, are not mandatory.

14

The main ingredients

Playroom accommodation

45. This is the core of the nursery and must cater for a wide range of groups and activities with varying space needs.

  a. Activities such as storytelling and listening, looking at books, small music groups and resting require small spaces with some degree of enclosure, such as quiet rooms or bays.
  b. Large scale activities (movement, larger music groups, boisterous play involving climbing, swinging, jumping and rolling) require large open spaces. They may also take place outside.
  c. Activities such as painting, cutting and modelling need mainly tables and benches.
  d. Large projects and work with building blocks require clear floor space.
  e. Imaginative role playing; home play and dressing up require bays and corners off the main activity area.
  f. Messy activities, such as play with sand, water and clay and caring for pets, are ideally located in a perimeter area close to a sink, with easy access to the external covered area which may also be used for these activities.
  g. A suitable area is needed which can be cleared for lunch for the few children who attend full time.

46. Most activities are not confined to hard and fast zones within the nursery but move and develop according to need. However, some areas, such as quiet rooms and bays, do need greater permanence and the design should allow for a clear progression from quiet to noisy activities and from clean to messy ones. Opportunities are needed for discussion between adults and individual children or small groups of two or three children. Group sizes may vary from such small "pastoral" groups to larger groups of perhaps twenty children with several adults.

47. The original cellular structure of the Blidworth and Carlton nurseries provides a variety of linked but separate spaces (see figures 5 and 6), which are capable of further subdivision to create activity areas. This arrangement successfully reduces the overall scale and minimises disturbance between activities, but some additional openings between spaces were introduced to simplify supervision. In contrast, the linear form of the space at Glenbrook poses few problems for supervision (see figure 7), and encourages the children to explore the whole nursery but makes it less easy to achieve a satisfactory separation between activities. In the case of the sixty place Clifton nursery (see figure 8), the large "L" shaped space may be subdivided to provide for two units either of thirty or of twenty and forty.

Clifton Whitegate

15

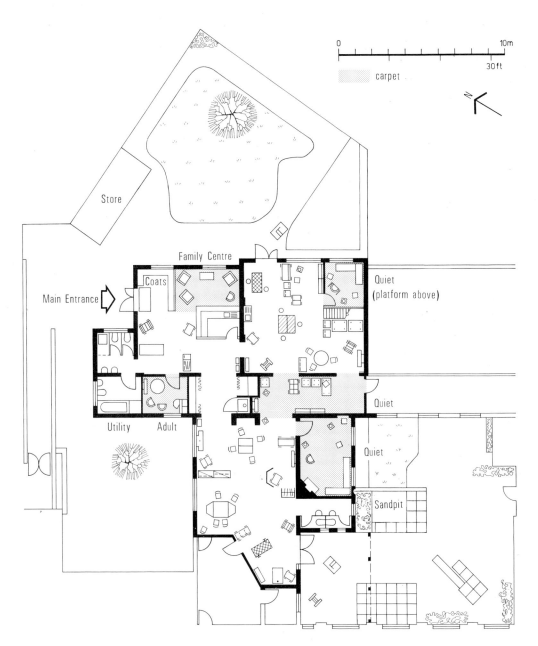

5. Blidworth: plan of nursery unit

Quiet Bays

48. Bays off the main activity area may be used by a small group of children listening to a story, set out for imaginative play or used as a rest area. There will often be small residual spaces in converted buildings which can be exploited to provide such enclaves. Thus at Glenbrook a small porch forms a restricted but distinctive space, at Blidworth the corridor section between the two main areas provides a contrast in scale and finish and at Clifton a bay was provided by opening up an existing store to the activity area.

Temporary bays may be formed by using furniture and equipment.

Quiet Rooms

49. These share many of the characteristics and uses of the bays but except for vision panels are completely enclosed. The seclusion and intimacy offered is especially important for new arrivals who may need to be introduced gradually to the wider social world of the nursery. In many older schools such as Carlton and Blidworth, with their large, high-ceilinged rooms,

16

there may be very few such spaces readily available. At these schools a small enclosed box was provided within the activity area. A stair gives access to the roof of the box which is carpeted for quiet play. At Glenbrook two quiet rooms were provided as part of the new extension.

Meals
50. Lunch for the few children who may be full-time is supplied from the main school kitchen (except in the case of Carlton where meals are delivered from a central kitchen). It is served in a suitable part of the activity area from the servery in the Family Centre which also provides hot drinks.

51. The area per place of playroom accommodation (including quiet rooms but excluding adult rooms, teaching storage and the outside-play room at Carlton) in the four nurseries was as follows:

Blidworth	(40 place)	3.2 m²
Clifton	(60 place)	2.9 m²
Carlton	(40 place)	2.7 m²
Glenbrook	(40 place)	2.6 m²

These areas are well above both the statutory minimum area of 2.3 m² per child and that provided in new nursery units in Nottinghamshire. It is rarely possible in conversion projects to match available space with the minimum area required for the playroom accommodation. However, ancillary areas in the four projects are no larger than they would be in an equivalent new building.

Outside-Play Room
52. In order to compensate for the inadequacy of the outside play space at Carlton an additional indoor space has been provided. This is different in character from the other nursery spaces and is intended to provide for noisier and more boisterous activities. It leads directly to the covered outside space.

Coat Areas
53. Besides providing for the storage of outdoor clothes the coat areas are the focal point for arrival and departure. These occasions are significant because they provide a natural opportunity for parents and nursery staff to meet. The relationship of the coat area

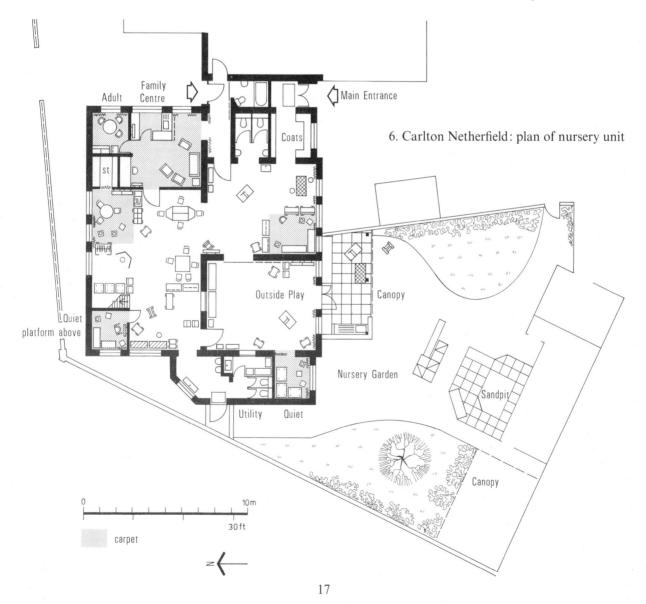

6. Carlton Netherfield: plan of nursery unit

0   10m
30 ft

carpet

17

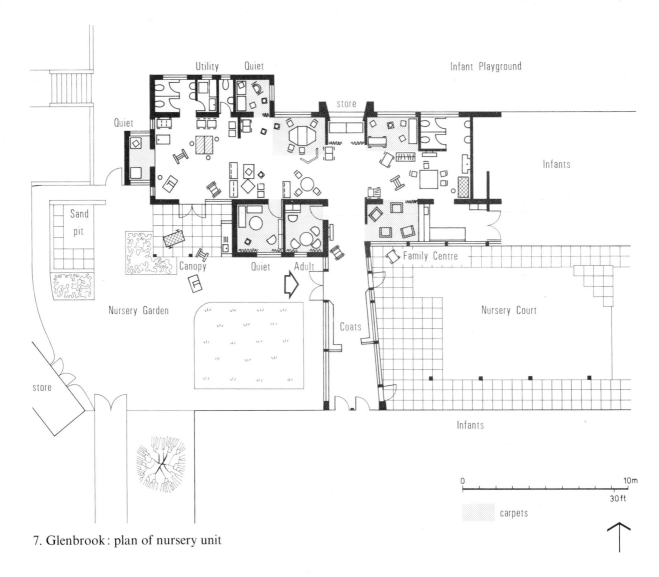

Utility   Quiet   Infant Playground

store

Quiet

Sand
pit   Infants

Canopy   Quiet   Adult

Nursery Garden   Family Centre

Coats   Nursery Court

store

Infants

0   10m

30 ft

carpets

7. Glenbrook: plan of nursery unit

to the rest of the nursery is therefore important. While it should clearly be near the entrance, it should also be easy to supervise and capable of absorbing overspill from the activity area so that both parents and children may be drawn naturally into the nursery activities. The coat areas at Clifton and Blidworth meet these aims well. At Carlton the area links the main entrance and the activity area but is effectively only a lobby where floor play would be difficult. The coat area at Glenbrook, being much larger, would encourage floor play but is somewhat isolated from the activity area.

Lavatories and Utility Rooms

54. Easy supervision of the lavatories by staff from the main area of the nursery is important and the lavatories should therefore be close to the activity area and not separated from it by doors or lobbies. In each project two sets of lavatories are provided. These are domestic in scale and well distributed although in one or two cases a little isolated from the activity area. The relationship of lavatories to activity area is best at Glenbrook where the existing services allowed greatest flexibility in arrangement.

55. A utility room containing a linen cupboard, sink, washing machine and clothes drier is also provided. A hand shower and raised shower tray or large sink is located close to the lavatory area within the Utility Room in three projects where, to avoid embarrassment, children can be washed in privacy after accidents. At Carlton and Blidworth a bathroom has been provided as part of the Family Centre; this includes a staff lavatory.

Adult Room

56. There is a separate room in each nursery near the entrance for use by the staff for meeting parents and other visitors to the nursery; at other times this can serve as a quiet room.

Family Centre

57. At Blidworth, Carlton and Glenbrook small Family Centres have been provided. Their purpose is to enable the community, and especially parents, to participate in the work of the nursery and the school as a whole and to encourage the better use of school facilities for the mutual benefit of school and community. It follows that the centre should be closely

18

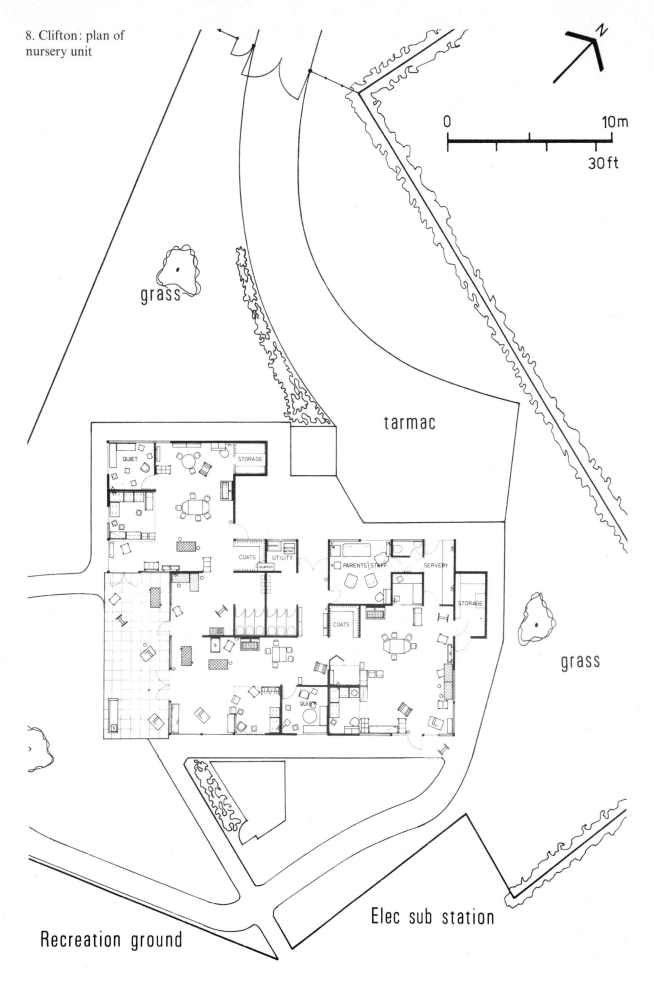

8. Clifton: plan of
nursery unit

N

0   10m

30ft

grass

tarmac

QUIET

STORAGE

COATS   SHOWER   WASHING MACHINE

UTILITY

CALORIFIER

PARENTS\STAFF

SERVERY

STORAGE

COATS

QUIET

grass

Recreation ground

Elec sub station

Clifton Whitegate

related to the nursery but also near the entrance and capable of use out of school hours as its use will not be confined purely to the parents of nursery children. The cost of furnishing and equipping these centres was met by funds provided under the Urban Programme.

58. Each centre consists of a snack bar run by parents and staff with a servery and an associated sitting area. This servery may also be used to dispense lunch for those attending the nursery full-time. There is provision for making and mending toys and equipment, and for the display of information and work. There is also space for the babies in prams and the "toddlers" who may accompany parents. For these children, an early introduction through the Family Centre will greatly ease their eventual entry into the nursery. At Blidworth and Glenbrook it has been possible to integrate the Family Centres fully into the nurseries, while maintaining a close relationship to the entrance and nursery garden. At Carlton the Centre is rather more isolated, but has the advantage of a separate entrance. No Family Centre is provided at Clifton as it is anticipated that these facilities will be developed in the main building. Instead the adult room serves as a social area for parents and staff.

External Areas
59. In designing for nursery education, the planning

20

60. Verandahs at all four nurseries are similarly constructed of opaque plastic sheeting with translucent panels supported by timber rafters on steel posts. They are kept as low as possible (2.1 m) to give better protection from the elements and to provide a scale sympathetic to the children; at Blidworth and Clifton they are accommodated in existing recesses.

61. In each project the hard play area includes a general space for using large stationary equipment and a circuit for riding or running around with paths wide enough for wheeled toys to pass each other. A grassed area is also provided, usually mounded, and planted with trees and shrubs with space for growing flowers. The sand-pit forms a major focal point for outside play and is therefore positioned near the verandah and provided with access from the hard play area. Adjacent to each hard play area is a spacious and easily accessible store for large items of play equipment. At Blidworth and Glenbrook these take the form of second-hand railway box cars (5.5 × 2.1 m) removed from their chassis and painted in bright colours.

62. At Carlton and Blidworth, where existing external areas were treeless and entirely hard, it was particularly important to improve the external environment. Substantial sections of tarmac have been removed to provide space for grass, trees and shrubs. At Glenbrook, where adjacent areas were mainly grass, additional hard play space has been provided. Some additional paths and a second set of entrance gates were provided at Clifton allowing an existing parking area to be used as a hard play space. At Blidworth and Glenbrook the nursery garden has had to be divided between an external area and an internal courtyard and this poses problems for supervision. On the other hand the courtyards offer a secure environment and may in the future be developed as important links with the infant schools. It is hoped that staff and parents will gradually add to the planting and equipment at all the nurseries by self-help.

of the building cannot be separated from that of the outside play area[1]. The building and its surroundings should be treated as an integrated whole with as direct a transition as possible from the inside to the outside and easy access from the activity area to a verandah. This will be used for a wide variety of activities from sand and water play to work at tables and easels and may also accommodate cages for pets. It should be provided with a sink and cold water tap.

---

[1]Fuller descriptions of the requirements for outdoor play spaces are given in Design Note 1: Building for Nursery Education and in "A Right to be Children; Designing for the education of the under fives".

Design of internal spaces

63. As they existed, the main internal spaces at Carlton and Blidworth were high and gaunt and this made them very unsympathetic to their new use as nurseries. The original high window sills had useful wall surfaces below them but tended to isolate the nursery from outside. A number of window sills were therefore lowered and some glazed external doors added. At Clifton where the converse was true and glazing was excessive it was relatively easy to replace glazed panels with solid to provide additional wall surfaces. Apart from these small alterations, it was decided to rely mainly on the use of colour and finishes to achieve the necessary change of the scale and character of spaces.

Use of colour and finishes

64. A single colour scheme is designed to run throughout each nursery (see figure 9). Quiet areas, lavatories, storage and coat areas are differentiated in some small way. To reduce the visual scale interest is concentrated on the lower part of the walls. A cornice line in the form of a painted band is established to coincide with the tops of doors and other openings; at Carlton and Blidworth this band incorporates the exposed warm-air distribution ducts. Above the band walls and ceilings are painted in light colours. The walls below the band are painted in strong colours and all curtains, pin up and chalk surfaces are arranged to stop at the lower edge of the band. At a lower level, there generally is a timber dado rail, coloured to echo the high level band. This is sometimes interrupted by pin up and chalk surfaces which extend to the skirting. In most cases light fittings have been lowered to coincide with the level of the upper band and imply a lowered ceiling height. In the quiet rooms and some of the bays

a hessian wall covering has been used to provide a warm domestic ambience.

Floor finishes
65. Except in a few areas, where existing timber or vinyl-tiled floors were retained, foam backed vinyl sheet is used throughout in a single light colour and pattern. This encourages a flexible use of all the space available. In contrast a soft foam backed carpet of wool/rayon mix is used in the quiet rooms and as loose carpeting in the general areas.

Acoustics
66. Because Carlton and Blidworth are older buildings with high ceilings and hard reverberant surfaces it proved necessary to increase the area of sound absorbent materials such as carpets, curtains and soft wall coverings. In the outside play room at Carlton where acoustic conditions were particularly difficult a system of cheap and simple sound absorbing baffles has been designed to be fixed to the ceiling (see Appendix C).

9. Blidworth: section through playroom

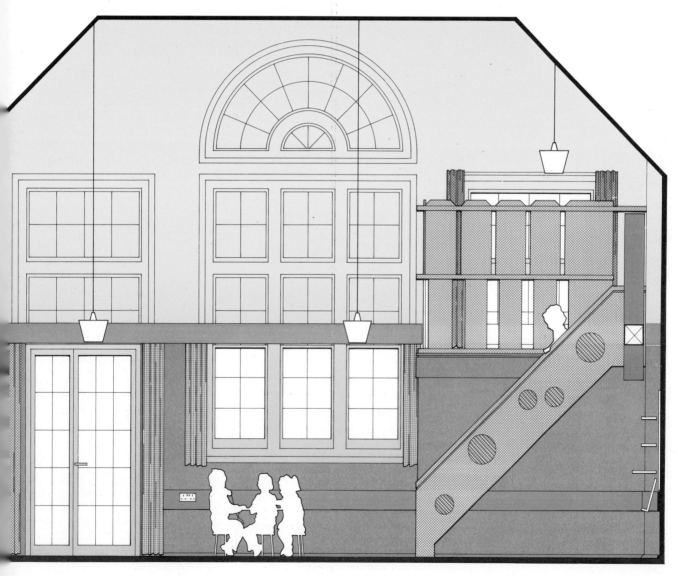

Furniture and equipment

67. A co-ordinated range of loose furniture and equipment in sizes appropriate to their users has been provided to meet the wide variety of requirements for work and play in the nurseries[1]. Figure 10 shows the typical heights of furniture and fittings and their relationship to the wall treatments described in paragraph 64. In selecting items particular attention was paid to their versatility and flexibility. Although all four nurseries had broadly similar requirements the details of the selection for each were influenced to some extent by the individual character of its building.

Sketches and brief descriptions of the items provided and a complete furniture schedule can be found in Appendix D.

68. A number of the items provided have been developed especially for use in nurseries. These include the upholstered seating cube, for use in quiet areas and on carpets, tray carts, which are mobile trolleys containing eight plastic trays allowing access and storage display at the child's level, and the sand or water trolley which can be used inside or outside and moved easily for storage. Two new trolleys, for miscellaneous items and dressing-up materials respec-

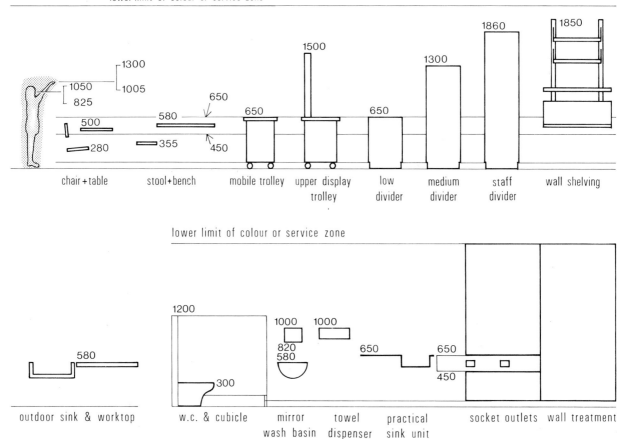

10. Relationships of furniture and fittings

---

[1]Information on the anthropometric requirements of nursery age children is given in Building Bulletin 38: School Furniture Dimensions: Standing and Reaching.

tively, were developed for the project and provide additional display and storage on a scale appropriate to the nursery child. Figure 11 shows the items mentioned in this paragraph. Sketches of all the items of furniture provided can be found in Appendix D.

Storage

69. Each of the four projects has one or more strategically placed walk-in stores, with a total area of around 0.1m² per place, for the bulk storage of materials and equipment. Loose furniture provides local storage—in particular for items in daily use such as books and kits which need to be directly accessible for the children—and is also used to subdivide teaching areas and provide additional display surfaces. A proportion of teaching storage is mobile to allow easy repositioning. Storage has also been provided for the personal belongings of children and staff.

2.4 Upholstered Seat Cube

5.1 Tray Cart

5.2 Small Service Trolley

5.5 Sand or Water Trolley

5.7 Dressing Up Trolley

11. Nursery furniture

Services

70. During the life of a building the condition of services may deteriorate to the point where further alteration is impossible. For this reason, and because of a need for higher environmental standards, it is often necessary in conversion work to undertake substantial renewal of services installations. The cost of services will therefore tend to be high as a proportion of total cost.

Drainage and water supply

71. In older schools such as Blidworth and Carlton water storage may be very limited. When additional fittings are introduced water authorities will often demand a substantial increase in capacity and the location and support of new water tanks can create difficulties. At Blidworth it was possible to install a tank at high level in the ceiling space but at Carlton a separate supporting structure was necessary. Some additional drainage was required in all the projects. To avoid breaking into concrete ground floor slabs new drains were run outside the building wherever possible.

Sanitary fittings

72. Water closets and washbasins for pupils are provided on the scale of one per ten (in accordance with statutory requirements). Other fittings provided include:

—play sinks
—servery sinks
—utility/shower sinks
—baths
—adult WCs and wash basins.

The hot water supply to play sinks and showers is controlled to a maximum temperature[1]. Play sinks are dispersed throughout the nurseries served by a local water heater and wash basins are supplied by spray taps for reasons of economy.

Lighting

73. It was thought that the warmer and more domestic character of tungsten lighting was most appropriate for the nurseries. The existing installations at Clifton and Blidworth have therefore been substantially retained and a new tungsten system has been installed at Glenbrook where the original system was inadequate for the new use of the rooms.

74. At Carlton, the oldest of the four schools, the original lighting installation had been replaced with fluorescent fittings. Most of these have been retained

Glenbrook

but lowered to the level of the painted cornice. A few tungsten fittings have been introduced in the more intimate areas. In all the projects lowered lights or spotlights are used to enhance the character of such spaces as the Quiet Rooms, Bays and Snack Bars and to provide a contrast with the main activity area.

75. Relatively few socket outlets are provided in the main nursery areas and these are mainly for routine cleaning and maintenance. A number are provided in Snack Bars for items of equipment such as small ovens and electric kettles.

Space heating
76. At Clifton Whitegate the existing gas fired convector heaters were quite adequate and have been retained. At Carlton and Blidworth, as at many other older schools, heating was by hospital pattern radiators served by large diameter (150 mm) cast iron pipes. Such systems are technically difficult to adapt, severely limit the amount of usable wall space at low level and tend to work to higher surface temperatures than are desirable in a nursery[1]. Temperatures cannot be reduced nor the radiators and pipes satisfactorily guarded without reducing the heat output of what may already be an inadequate system. At Glenbrook there was no heating system in the ancillary accommodation available for conversion, and that serving the rest of the school could not be extended as the boiler was already working to capacity. In these three cases therefore, it was decided to install a new gas fired ducted warm air system to serve the nursery only. This system has four significant advantages:

—it frees wall and floor space where it is most needed
—it provides a rapid warm-up and is flexible in use
—it presents no exposed hot surfaces
—it is relatively low in installation and running cost.

At Carlton and Blidworth the distribution ducts and outlet grills are positioned at door head height. At Glenbrook, the ducts are located immediately beneath the ceiling with short drops to outlet grilles.

Ventilation
77. Lavatories and utility rooms are well ventilated, either naturally, as at Blidworth, Glenbrook and Clifton, or artificially by carefully placed extract fans as at Carlton.

---

[1] DES Environmental Guidelines recommend a maximum of 43°C.

Future development of the schools

78. In the development plans described below the aim has not been to provide a detailed design for the future of each school, because needs and conditions may change in the future and staffing ratios and group sizes cannot be predicted, but rather to provide a broad framework for co-ordinating growth and change. Such plans must be flexible but they should at least ensure that the main priorities are kept in view and that whatever resources are available are used to the best advantage.

Glenbrook

79. The linear form of the Glenbrook building makes it particularly difficult to adapt to changing needs. The installation of the nursery isolated one of the existing infant classrooms and it was therefore necessary to provide an additional covered link direct to the rest of the infant school. The addition of the nursery and the construction of this link constitute the first phase of the development plan.

80. In 1975 when the investigation was begun the infant school roll stood at 165. Through a general revision of catchment areas of all the primary schools in the Bilborough area, the authority hopes to maintain this number despite the decline in the birthrate but would aim to be able to accommodate 240 pupils if the birthrate increases once more. The final development plan (see figure 12a) is therefore based on eight groups of thirty children to be accommodated in the southern spine of classrooms, with a gross area per place of approximately 5.2 m² and a teaching area per place of 3.3 m² (including the very large hall). Some of the partitions between the existing classrooms would be removed to allow more flexibility in the use of space and the resulting linked areas furnished to provide home bases for general teaching with access to shared practical spaces in the cross links and, through verandahs, to the courtyards. The second spine would contain the nursery, the lavatories ancillary to the infant rooms, the music room (already converted by self help) and some community accommodation. The separate halls for PE and dining would remain.

81. As infant numbers are likely to remain at around 160 for a number of years to come, in the interim stage of the development plan it is proposed that one of the classrooms should be retained for use by the nursery as an outside-play room, as shown in figure 12b.

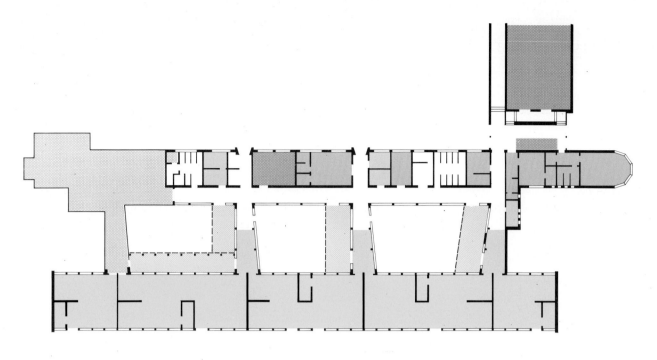

12a. Glenbrook: a suggested plan for the future development of the infant and nursery school

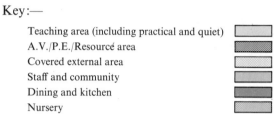
12b. An interim stage in the development of the infant and nursery school pending an increase in the size of the infant school roll

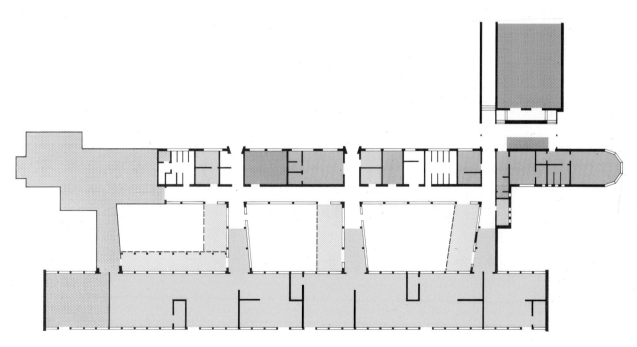

Robert Jones Infant and Junior Schools

82. Because it was anticipated that the additional classroom would not be available until 1978–79 the nursery project was originally planned in two phases. However in the event the classroom was released earlier and both phases were completed at the same time. In 1975 at the time of the investigation the infant roll stood at 235. By 1977 it was expected to decline to 190 and eventually in the two years that followed to 140.

83. The final phase of the development plan at Blidworth provides for nine groups of junior children and four or five groups of infant children (see figure 13). Teaching area per place is approximately 2.8 m² including hall and resource area and gross area per place is around 5.0 m². Some new building is proposed in the form of an extension across the internal court which will house dining facilities and a resource area, and will also act as a link between the infant and junior school. A number of new outside covered areas would be added and the remaining tarmac areas around the perimeter of building would be further developed and related to the existing nursery garden.

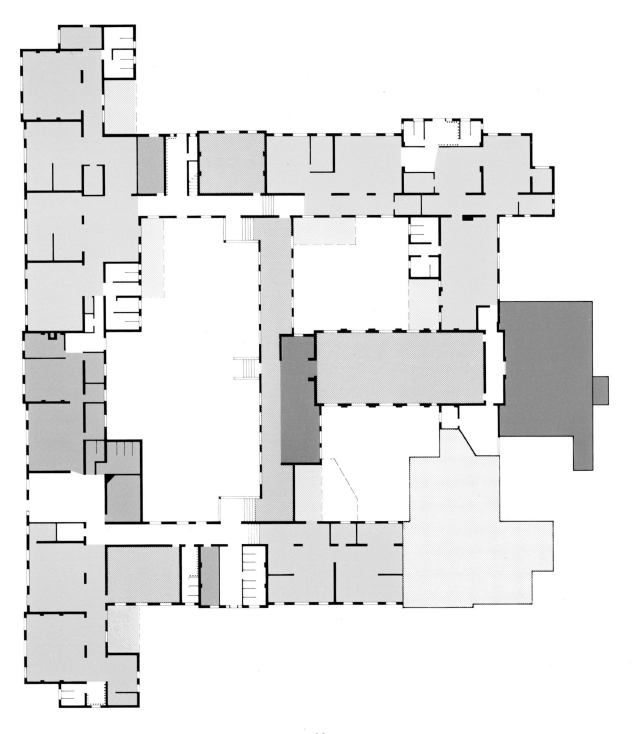

Robert Jones Infant and
Junior School

13. Blidworth: a suggested plan for the future
development of the infant and nursery school

Key:— Teaching area (including practical and quiet)
Â.V./P.E./Resource area
Covered external area
Staff and community
Dining and kitchen
Nursery

Carlton Netherfield

84. In 1975 the infant school roll stood at 240. It was forecast that this would reach a peak of 266 in 1977–78 followed by a decline to 220 by 1980–81. The first stage of the development plan includes the provision of the forty place nursery and nursery garden with the rest of the old infant building occupied by a group of thirty infant children in each of the three remaining classrooms and a resource area in the wide entrance hall. The main hall is used for music and movement and dining. The old junior school contains the other six groups of thirty and the new internal lavatories. The hall is used for PE by the whole school.

85. In the second stage of the development plan the nine classrooms would be altered to provide home bases with shared practical areas for seven groups, while the hall in the old infant building would be used for music and movement with a dining area at one end. Gross area per place, including halls, is approximately 4.5 m² with teaching area approximately 3.0 m² per place. The lavatories in the former junior school which were provided in Stage I would be extended and new lavatories provided in the former infant building. The existing caretaker's house would be converted to provide staff accommodation and a head teacher's office, allowing the temporary staff hut to be removed (see figure 14).

86. An important aspect of the development plan is the improvement of the external areas. The site would gradually be opened up by the removal of external lavatories and other extraneous buildings and additional planting would be introduced.

87. The value of the development plan at Carlton was demonstrated at a very early stage in the design of the nursery project. A small sum was allocated to provide some additional internal lavatories for the infant school and it was possible to position these to the best advantage for the future development of the whole school.

Clifton Whitegate

88. Unlike the other three projects the nursery unit at Clifton is isolated from the main school. No major development is contemplated in the future, although it is hoped that with the help of the local community there can be continuing small improvements both to the building and to the site. A recent example has been the decoration of some of the external wall panels of the building by the art department of the local comprehensive school.

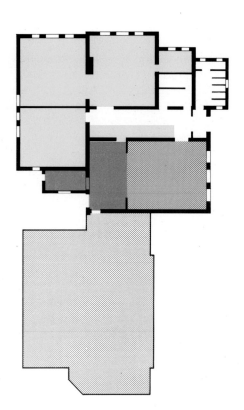

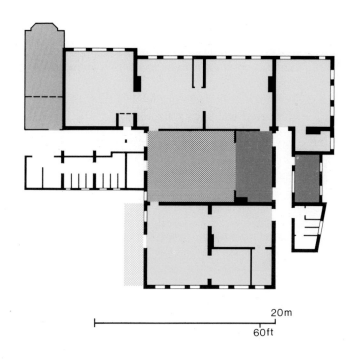

20m
60ft

14. Carlton Netherfield: a suggested plan for the future development of the infant and nursery school

Key:—

Teaching area (including practical and quiet)
A.V./P.E./Resource area
Covered external area
Staff and community
Dining and kitchen
Nursery

Cost and Contractual Arrangements

89. The financial objectives of the project were three fold;

    a. to cost plan the projects so as to provide the best value for money within the overall budget;

    b. to provide more general information on the range of costs likely to be met within conversion work;

    c. to compare the costs of the projects with those of an equivalent new building.

Main factors in cost of conversion

90. The cost of adapting space in an existing building for another use can vary greatly. Generally the more fundamental the change of use the more costly is the conversion. The factors likely to be most influential in determining cost are as follows:

(a) the extent of major structural alterations or additions. In only one of the projects (Glenbrook) were there substantial extensions to the building. In the others structural alterations were confined to the formation of additional openings between adjacent spaces and to lowering the height of some window sills to give a better view to the outside;

(b) the need for alterations or extensions to existing services (in particular to drainage and heating systems). In the case of older buildings where heating systems use large diameter cast iron pipes, replacement of a complete section with a new independent system may be necessary. Electrical systems are usually more suited to piece-meal adaptation but again, if the system is old, renewal may be necessary;

(c) work necessary to enable displaced activities to be relocated. This will depend upon the particular circumstances and, if at all extensive, could bring into question the viability of a project. Such work was needed in only two of the projects (Blidworth and Glenbrook);

(d) the extent of essential repairs required to the existing structure. This too could bring into question the viability of a project. In the case of the Nursery Projects all four buildings were in reasonably good condition and only normal maintenance was required.

Cost planning and control

91. A cost plan and a provision allocation based upon its particular needs was prepared for each project. It was agreed that there should be virement between projects throughout the pre-contract stage. It was then possible to confirm that the broad objectives of the projects could be met within the overall budget established earlier by the authority. In the case of three of the projects (Carlton Netherfield, Blidworth and Glenbrook) the allocation included sums made available from the Urban Programme to provide accommodation for community use. Allowance was also made for the cost of any reaccommodation work and for a generous contingency sum (around 8% of the contract total) to cover the unknown factors of conversion work. It was recognised that services were likely to be a much higher proportion of total cost than in new work and that it was important to have early and continued specialist advice on the design and costing of the services element. Once building work had commenced costs were carefully monitored against the framework of the cost plans.

Contractual arrangements

92. Although the four projects differed somewhat in scope and were in different areas, it was felt that there would be cost and contractual advantages if they were tendered and managed as a group rather than as individual projects. However if these advantages were to be secured, the tendering method had to allow some choice to the contractor. It was therefore decided to allow a tenderer to opt for the three projects in the Nottingham area as a group, for Blidworth only, or for all four projects. In the event the successful contractor opted for the last alternative.

93. In these projects, as in all conversion work taking place in occupied buildings, it was particularly important to establish a detailed programme for the work on site in consultation with the user. Spaces had to be vacated well in advance of building operations and where reaccommodation work was necessary this had to be carried out prior to commencement of the main project. Access for the contractor was needed during all normal working hours and an adequate area for the contractors' use had to be fenced off.

Value for money

94. A simplified analysis of the cost on tender of the four nurseries is given in Appendix B. For the purposes of comparison this includes a cost analysis for an equivalent new unit in Nottingham. The cost per place and per unit area in the four projects is compared below with the cost in an equivalent new Nottinghamshire standard nursery unit (prices based on the then current serial contract).

34

	Cost per place	cost per m²	% of cost of place in new bldg.	% of cost per m² in new bldg.	Cost per place in new bldg [1].	Cost per m² in new bldg[1].
Clifton (60 place)	£263	57.08	45%	27%	£586	213
Carlton (40 place)	£491	91.27	61%	33%	£809	277
Blidworth (40 place)	£525	112.35	65% (59%[2])	41%	£809	277
Glenbrook (40 place)	£686	191.83	85% (79%[2])	69%	£809	277

[1]assuming flat site and reasonably available services.
[2]if cost of reaccommodation work is excluded.

Building work began in April 1976 and was completed in December 1976.

Glenbrook

95. These figures show a considerable variation in cost between individual projects, the most expensive costing more than twice as much per place as the cheapest, but the former still compares favourably with the cost of new building. Such variation is inevitable because the cost of conversion depends very much on the opportunities and problems which particular buildings present. In considering value for money it may therefore be better to think of an average cost per place over a group of projects rather than in terms of individual projects. In the case of the Nottinghamshire projects this is £466, or 63% of the cost of providing the place in an equivalent new building in Nottinghamshire and around 52% of the average cost per place of new nursery buildings in England and Wales in 1975–76.

96. The Nottinghamshire projects do not of course represent the full range of costs which might be incurred in conversion work. In very favourable circumstances a satisfactory nursery unit might be provided for little more than the cost of redecorating and refurnishing some recently built accommodation. On the other hand a project involving substantial structural alterations and extensions could still represent good value for money when compared with the new equivalent. Clearly therefore this parcel of projects may not be representative for the country as a whole; in other cases with a more favourable "mix" of buildings costs could be lower.

97. So much for capital cost. Running costs in the converted Nottinghamshire accommodation should be little different from those in new purpose-built units. However, for a new building the whole expense of running and maintaining it is an additional cost which the maintaining authority has to bear. For a conversion, given that it is housed in otherwise surplus accommodation which could not simply be taken out of use, much of the maintenance and running cost would be incurred anyway. In terms of recurrent costs therefore conversion has a clear advantage over new buildings.

Conclusions

98. This Bulletin has described how the team sought to achieve the objectives set for the project (see paragraph 13). It is felt that the central purpose of providing a range of educational opportunities equivalent to that offered by a new, purpose-built nursery unit was fulfilled. Where some of the convenience of purpose-built nurseries has had to be foregone, it is arguable that the greater area per pupil and the wider variety of spaces available will more than compensate for this. In addition, there are benefits to both nursery and infant school from the greater degree of integration possible with a conversion as compared with an "add-on" unit. All this has been achieved at a considerable saving in cost as compared with a new unit.

99. This is a significant result in relation to the prospects for nursery education building over the next five years. In this period public expenditure constraints will inevitably restrict the allocation of resources to new nursery building—which makes it all the more important to make the best use of what resources are available. At the same time primary school rolls will fall sharply; at present there are 4.7 million pupils at primary schools in England and Wales and the figure projected for 1982 is 3.8 m. This should mean that many more primary schools will have surplus space available for conversion where resources permit. It is hoped that this Bulletin has helped to demonstrate the potential of such space.

Glenbrook

37

Appendices

Appendix A
Nurseries Visited During Investigation[1]

Lane Head Nursery School, Walsall (as in 1975)

Conversion of an old primary school, built in 1880, into a sixty place (full-time equivalent) nursery school.

Staff: head and one qualified teacher and four NNEB assistants (with a number of other auxiliaries).

Accommodation: the play area was very generous —over 5.0 m² per place. There were four distinct and largely separate spaces each with a different character. One room was virtually self-contained and had its own lavatories (it could be used for handicapped children); a second room was enclosed and carpeted and was used mainly for quiet domestic play and music; there was a larger open area used for creative activities. Finally there was an "indoor-outdoor" space with a translucent plastic roof and an indoor paddling pool; this space was used for water play and large scale messy activities. French windows led onto a raised terrace with a ramp down to the playground.

Outside: hard play area with a "play maze" created from an old block of outside lavatories; more grassed area was required.

A simple and effective conversion. The nursery was popular with a long waiting list and good relations with the parents; some mothers helped in the nursery.

Millfields Nursery School, Walsall (as in 1975)

Conversion of a primary school built in 1890 into a sixty place (full-time equivalent) nursery school.

Staff: head and one qualified teacher and four NNEB assistants (with one other auxiliary).

Accommodation: the play area amounted to 3.6 m² per place; there were five distinct but linked spaces each with a different character with varying ceiling

heights and floor finishes. As at Lane Head there was an enclosed and carpeted quiet room, and an "inside-outside" room with paddling pool.

Outside: tarmac with some trees and a "play maze" created once again from an old lavatory block.

As in the case of Lane Head, a simple and effective conversion.

Victoria Road Infant and Junior School, Walsall (as in 1975)

Conversion of former domestic science classrooms in a school built around 1910 into a forty place nursery unit.

Staff: four NNEB assistants (no qualified teacher).

Accommodation: this consisted of three large interconnecting rooms, a small office, a kitchen and a store. All three rooms were of rather similar character. One included a paddling pool.

Outside: play space was limited with a removable "ranch" fence for protection.

The school is now known as Salisbury County Primary School.

Delves Infant and Nursery School, Walsall (as in 1975)

Conversion of two classrooms, cloakroom and corridor in a 1937 Infants School to a forty place nursery unit.

Staff: one qualified teacher, three NNEB assistants (with a number of auxiliaries).

Accommodation: one room was mainly for domestic play, large scale floor play and table work. Bays for domestic play were very good with adult scale soft furniture. The second room was mainly for messy and creative activities, such as sand and water play. The corridor provided for sand and block play and gave access to the outside.

Outside: hard play area with sand pit, a climbing frame and a grassed area with hedges.

Montem Primary School, Islington (ILEA) (as in 1975)

Space for a forty place nursery unit created by the conversion of some ground floor accommodation with a new link extension. The conversion was part of a general remodelling of this 1895 three decker school.

Staff: one qualified teacher and one NNEB assistant (at the time of the visit there were only thirty children in attendance—mostly full-time).

---

[1]Other examples of nursery conversions may be found in "A Right to be Children; Designing for the education of the under fives" published by RIBA Publications Ltd.

Accommodation: the room in the old building was used for music and movement and had a raised platform over a bedstore and a Wendy House. The new link classroom was used for table work and painting. Both rooms had verandahs which led to external play spaces. An old outside WC had been converted to a toy store.

The school was used after hours from 3.30 to 6.00 as a local play centre. There was also a family club room 6–7.30 for parents and children.

Laycock Primary School, Islington (ILEA) (as in 1975)

Conversion of ground floor space in a three-decker school dating from 1915 to provide a nursery unit for thirty-one full-time children (at the time of the visit).

Staff: one teacher and one assistant.

Accommodation: two rooms in the original building with small new extension with low window sills and french doors gave access to outside play space. The smaller room was used for music and movement and the larger, together with the extension, was used for table work and messy activities and accommodated a Wendy House. Outside the nursery had a small wired-off tarmac compound with a swing, a park bench and barrels with flowers.

Henry Fawcett Primary School, Lambeth (ILEA) (as in 1975)

Conversion of ground floor space in an old multi-storey primary school to a thirty-five place nursery unit.

Staff: one qualified teacher, two assistants (with one student).

Accommodation: this consisted of two large classrooms connected by an arched opening in the dividing wall. One room had a home corner, and was also used for sand play, floor play and dressing up; it also housed rocking horses and a caravan. The second room was used for table work, painting, water play and cookery; it also had a "cosy" space and a book corner.

Outside: there was no verandah, and outside play space was very limited.

There was good integration between the infants school and the nursery and the school put particular emphasis on developing good relations with the parents. An upstairs junior cloakroom had been converted to an attractive parents' room where a mothers and toddlers group can meet.

Randal Cremer Primary School, Hackney (ILEA) (as in 1975)

The nursery was in two parts—one in converted space in the main school building (built in 1875) and the other in an annexe some distance away.

Main Nursery
Staff: one qualified teacher and one assistant.

Accommodation: two inter-connected rooms for twenty-five children; one was used for quieter activities and had a carpeted area for block play, a carpeted store corner and raised area over a bed store set out for domestic play. The other room was used for messy and wet activities, table work and painting.

Outside play space was very limited.

The school was used as a play centre after school hours.

Annexe
Staff: One teacher and two assistants.

Accommodation: this purpose-designed forty place nursery was part of a community centre on a housing estate. The play room was essentially one large space with a number of carpeted areas for block play, domestic play and dressing up and a story corner, and a large general area for messy and creative work.

Outside: nursery garden—about half of which was paved—with a slide.

Blagdon Road Nursery School, Reading (as in 1975)

Organisation: the school accepted children on a part-time, full-time or extended day basis according to individual family circumstances (there was a maximum of 20 extended day children). A few children arrived early between 8.00 and 8.30 am and were served a simple breakfast. At 8.45 most of the other children arrived and dispersed to their areas throughout the three buildings; lunch was at 11.30 for those staying for the afternoon session which ran from 1.15 to 3.30. About 20 children stayed on after this and congregated for "family" tea in the main building, and then watched television or played. They were collected by their parents from 4.30 onwards. The school was open throughout the year and only closed for Bank Holidays and for one week at Christmas.

Staff: staffing arrangements were rather complex to allow for an extended day. There were six qualified teachers (Head, Deputy Head and four full-time teachers) and seven NNEB Assistants and students.

Appendix B

ANALYSIS OF COST ON TENDER FOR THE FOUR NURSERIES AND AN EQUIVALENT NEW UNIT

	CLIFTON		CARLTON	
Places Gross Area (excluding family centre) Tender Date	60 276m² March 76		40 215m² March 76	
BRIEF COST ANALYSIS	Total cost in £	Cost per m² gross floor area	Total cost in £	Cost per m² gross floor area
Substructure extension				
Superstructure extension				
Structural alterations and additions (including verandah)	4239	15.36	5838	27.15
Internal finishes (including WC partitions)	2546	9.22	2291	10.66
Fittings (including chair rail, pinboard, cupboard shelving etc)	1936	7.01	1373	6.39
Services (including drawings)	3442	12.47	7550	35.11
External works	2814	10.20	801	3.73
Reaccommodation work				
Contingency	777	2.82	1769	8.23
Total for Nursery	15754	57.08	19622	91.27
Family Centre (Urban Programme)			1114	
Contract Total	15754		20736	
Amount of preliminaries included in contract total	620		620	

Appendix C
Acoustic Treatment at
Carlton Netherfield

1. Because the school site at Carlton Netherfield was very restricted the nursery garden had to be limited in size. To compensate for this an indoor space was provided in which outdoor type activities could take place (see paragraph 52).

2. When this room was brought into use it became apparent that it suffered from two severe acoustic disadvantages. As in many Victorian schools the ceiling was very high (5 m) and the floor, which it was not economic to replace, was of good quality wood block. Using the Sabine formula and assuming an average occupancy of ten children the reverberation time was calculated at over two seconds; this meant that when children were engaged in their normal playing activities the room was intolerably noisy.

3. Because these problems are characteristic of Victorian schools a detailed investigation of the possible treatments was made. Of the alternatives a soft floor covering would have been inappropriate for the activities taking place in the space and would not have been sufficient as a sound absorber while a suspended ceiling would have been very expensive in view of the pendant light fittings, warm air ductwork and floor to ceiling windows which would have complicated the suspension system.

4. It was proposed therefore to suspend vertical absorbent panels from the ceiling in the horizontal plane of the light fittings with their lower edges about 2.6 m above floor level. It was anticipated that these panels, which have about 4.5 m² of absorbent area, will reduce the reverberation time to below 1 second. Reverberation times were measured before installation and will be measured again in due course.

5. Figure 1 shows the pattern in which the panels were set out. The actual layout is not critical but was developed to reduce the apparent number of panels, relieve monotony and allow as much daylight as possible to penetrate from the windows to the back of the room.

BLIDWORTH		GLENBROOK		NEW UNIT (WORKSOP)	
40 187m² March 76		40 143m² March 76		40 117m² January 76	
Total cost in £	Cost per m² gross floor area	Total cost in £	Cost per m² gross floor area	Total cost in £	Cost per m² gross floor area
		877 2910	6.13 20.35	2457 13216	20.96 112.96
3536	18.91	5504	38.49	262	2.24
1232	6.59	2367	16.55	included with superstructure	
1176 6683 3466 3021 1895 21009	6.29 35.74 18.53 16.16 10.13 112.35	840 7686 2771 2006 2470 27431	5.88 53.75 19.38 14.03 17.27 191.83	1077 501.1 8627 1725 32370	9.21 42.83 73.73 14.74 276.67
2197 24206		623 28054		 32370	
483		770		2274	

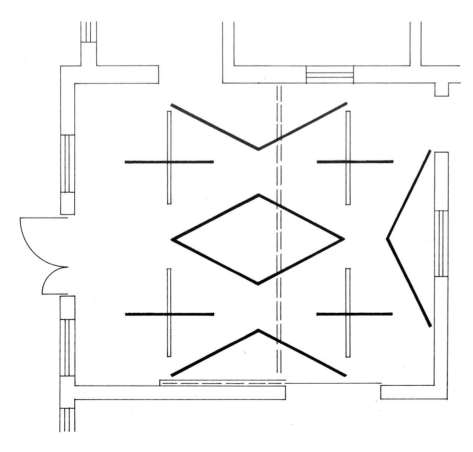

Figure 1. Plan showing disposition of absorbent panels
in indoor activity space.

Appendix D
Furniture and Fittings

1. This Appendix contains sketches and brief descriptions of each item of furniture provided for the nurseries together with a complete furniture schedule.

Seating
2. The main types of seating are as follows: (see also figure 11)

Chairs	— for grouping with tables and individual use;
Stools	— for use with standing height tables and benches;
Bench Seats	— upholstered benching for group seating in quiet areas; wooden benching in general spaces (may also be used as table surfaces);
Seat Cubes	— upholstered "soft" cubes used in quiet areas and on carpet squares; plastic cubes used as seats (and storage) indoors and outdoors;
Rocking Chairs	— for use in quiet areas;
Mattresses	— a foamed plastic core with waterproof cover to be used as seat, bed or as play equipment;
Adult Seats	— provided for staff and parents in quiet and general areas;
Easy Chairs	— provided in parent/staff social areas and some quiet rooms.

Table surfaces
3. A variety of table surfaces at sitting and standing height have been provided. These are listed below. All tables and benches are loose furniture and their positions can be determined by the staff.

Sitting Height	— Tables with linoleum tops in a variety of shapes and sizes to allow flexibility in use. These tables can be used for most nursery activities.
Standing Height (600 mm)	— Tables and benches with tops of melamine or hardboard for practical and messy activities. These surfaces are for indoor and outdoor use and may be easily moved within the nursery. At least one bench is provided in each nursery with a vice for elementary craft work.
Social	— Low coffee tables are provided in parent/staff areas.

Storage
4. As well as walk-in stores, storage for teaching materials and the personal belongings of staff and children has been provided.

Teaching storage:

Divider Units	— Low and medium height storage cupboards with full depth shelves open to both sides or with a back display panel;
Mobile Storage	— Storage trolleys on castors with shelves or plastic or wooden trays. Upper display panels of chalk board or pin up may be attached and this enhances their use as space dividers.

Personal Storage:

Staff Divider Units	— Lockable cupboards with hanging space or shelves for personal belongings;
Staff Work Stations	— A combined high level cupboard and writing shelf with pin board display surfaces;
Coat Storage	— Coat areas adjacent to main entrances have wall pegs with a fixed seat beneath.

General
5. This category contains items more specifically developed for nursery use. (See paragraph 68.)

Tray Cart	— a mobile trolley with eight plastic trays allowing access and display at the child's level;
Small Service Trolley	— a new item to provide shelves and trays for general storage allowing access and display for the children;
Book Box Trolley	— for the face display and storage of picture books and other materials (collage trolley);
Storage Cubes	— play boxes for display and storage, used in conjunction with block play;
Sand or Water Trolley	— for indoor and outdoor use by small groups of children; easily pushed through doors;
Folding Screens	— an aid to imaginative play; with the addition of dressing up materials they can become a Wendy House, shop etc;

Dressing up Trolley	— a new item for the storage of dressing up materials to a nursery scale;
Mobile Bins	— for the storage of all the paraphernalia of the nursery;
Easels	— for painting and display surfaces;
Shelf boxes	— used for creating raised areas for imaginative play or can be grouped together for display purposes.

The following sketches of items of furniture are numbered 2.1 to 5.10. These numbers relate to those in the schedule following.

2.1 Chairs	*2.2 Stools*	*2.3 Bench Seating*	*2.4 Seat Cubes*

Key symbol used in planning drawings

2.5 Adult Seating	*2.6 Rocking Chairs*	*2.7 Mattresses*

   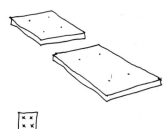

Key symbol used in planning drawings

2.8 Easy Chairs

Key symbol used in planning drawings

43

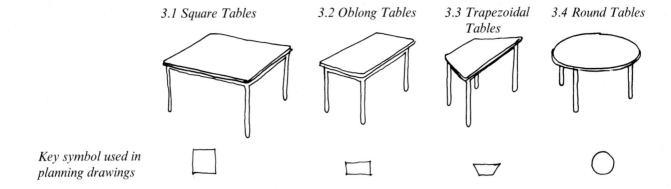

3.1 Square Tables *3.2 Oblong Tables* *3.3 Trapezoidal Tables* *3.4 Round Tables*

Key symbol used in planning drawings

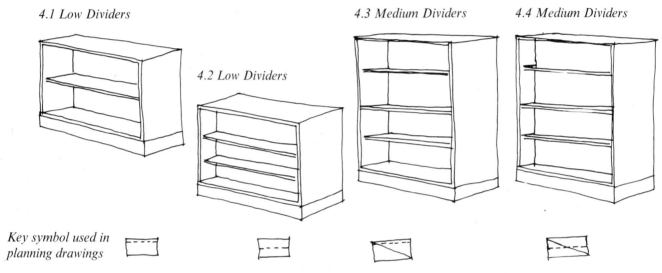

4.1 Low Dividers *4.2 Low Dividers* *4.3 Medium Dividers* *4.4 Medium Dividers*

Key symbol used in planning drawings

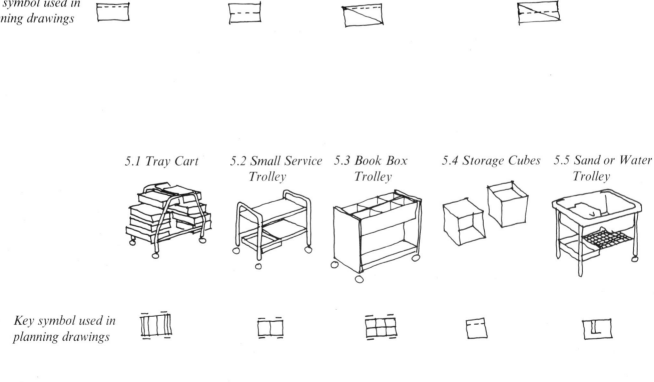

5.1 Tray Cart *5.2 Small Service Trolley* *5.3 Book Box Trolley* *5.4 Storage Cubes* *5.5 Sand or Water Trolley*

Key symbol used in planning drawings

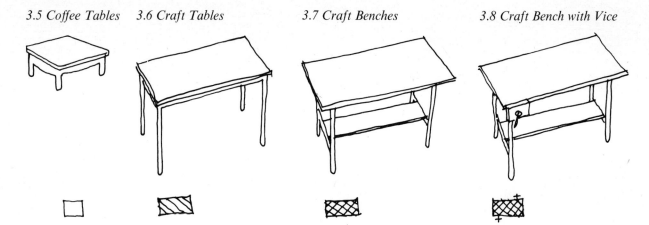

3.5 Coffee Tables   *3.6 Craft Tables*   *3.7 Craft Benches*   *3.8 Craft Bench with Vice*

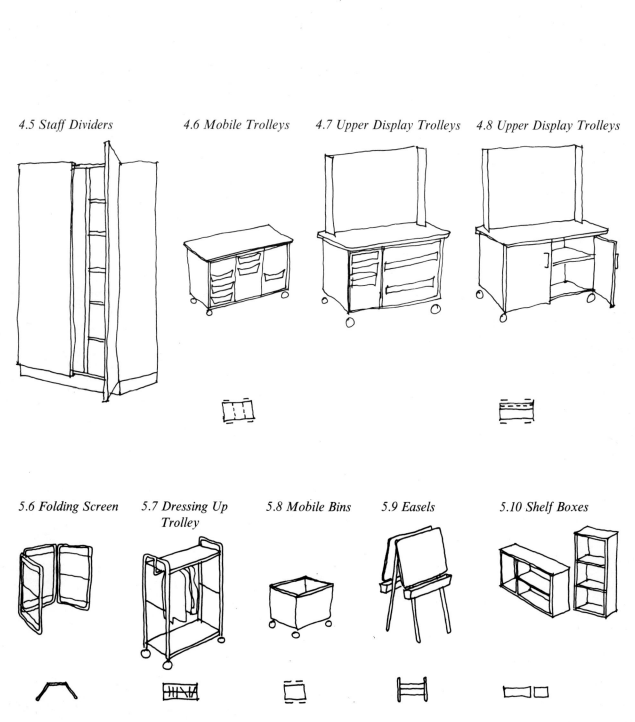

4.5 Staff Dividers   *4.6 Mobile Trolleys*   *4.7 Upper Display Trolleys*   *4.8 Upper Display Trolleys*

5.6 Folding Screen   *5.7 Dressing Up Trolley*   *5.8 Mobile Bins*   *5.9 Easels*   *5.10 Shelf Boxes*

Furniture schedule

Ref. No.		DIMENSIONS	CLIFTON 60 PLACES	BLIDWORTH 40 PLACES	CARLTON 40 PLACES	GLENBROOK 40 PLACES
	SEATING					
2.1	Chairs	× 280	20	12	12	12
2.2	Stools	× 355	8	6	4	6
2.3	Bench seats – upholstered	× 280	4	4	4	2
	Bench seats – wooden	× 280	2	3	2	1
2.4	Seat cubes – upholstered	300 × 300 × 250	6	6	6	6
	Seat cubes – plastic	300 × 300 × 250	9	6	6	6
2.5	Adult seats – chair	× 430	2	1	2	1
	Adult seats – armchair	× 430	2	4	4	4
2.6	Rocking chair	× 430	1	1	1	1
2.7	Mattresses – square	600 × 600 × 50	6	3	3	3
	Mattresses – oblong	900 × 600 × 50	6	3	3	3
2.8	Easy chair		3	3	3	4
	Settee		1	—	1	—
	WORKSURFACES					
3.1	Square	1100 × 1100 × 500	2	1	1	1
3.2	Oblong	1100 × 550 × 500	2	2	2	1
3.3	Trapezoidal	1100 × 550 × 500	4	2	2	2
3.4	Round	800 diam × 500	2	2	2	3
3.5	Coffee		1	1	1	—
3.6	Craft Table	1100 × 550 × 600	4	2	2	2
3.7	Craft Bench	1200 × 600 × 580	2	1	1	1
3.8	Craft Bench – with vices	1200 × 600 × 580	2	1	1	1
	STORAGE					
4.1	Divider – low level open shelves	980 × 450 × 650	1	1	1	1
4.2	– low level double sided	980 × 450 × 650	1	—	1	—
4.3	– medium level open shelves	980 × 450 × 1300	1	1	1	—
4.4	– medium level double sided	980 × 450 × 1300	1	1	1	1
4.5	– staff	980 × 450 × 1860	—	1	1	1
4.6	Mobile trolley	900 × 450 × 650	2	1	1	1
4.7	Mobile trolley – with upper display	1100 × 450 × 650	2	1	1	1
4.8	Mobile cupboard – with upper display	1100 × 450 × 650	1	1	1	1
	Staff locker unit	900 × 450 × 1270	2	1	1	1
	GENERAL					
5.1	Tray cart	680 × 460 × 535	3	3	3	2
5.2	Service trolley	750 × 450 × 580	1	2	2	2
5.3	Book box trolley	900 × 450 × 900	2	1	1	1
5.4	Storage Cube	450 × 450 × 450	6	4	6	4
5.5	Sand or Water trolley	600 × 900 × 580	4	2	3	2
5.6	Folding screen	600 × 450	1	1	1	1
5.7	Dressing up trolley	750 × 450 × 1240	1	1	1	1
5.8	Mobile bin	600 × 450	7	4	4	4
5.9	Easels	660 × 650 × 1130	4	2	2	3
5.10	Shelf boxes (set of 3)	900 × 450 × 225	3	2	2	—

Publications

Building Bulletins

PRIMARY SCHOOLS	Price Net
1. New Primary Schools (2nd edition (1972))	32p
3. Village Schools (1961)	50p
36. Development Project: Eveline Lowe Primary School (1967)	70p
47. Eveline Lowe School Appraisal (1972)	49p
53. Guillemont Junior School, Farnborough, Hampshire (1976)	£1.20

MIDDLE SCHOOLS

35. Problems in Schools Design: Middle Schools—Implications of Transfer at 12 or 13 years (1966)	£1.00

SECONDARY SCHOOLS

17. Development Project: Secondary School, Arnold (1960)	42½p
25. Secondary School Design: Sixth Form and Staff (1965)	£1.80
26. Secondary School Design: Physical Education (1965)	27½p
30. Secondary School Design: Drama and Music (1966)	70p
31. Secondary School Design: Workshop Crafts (1966)	40p
34. Secondary School Design: Designing for Art and Crafts (1967)	45p
39. Designing for Science: Oxford School Development Project (1967)	67½p
40. New Problems in School Design: Comprehensive Schools from Existing Buildings (1968)	80p
41. Sixth Form Centre, Rosebery County School for Girls (1968)	30p
43. Secondary School Design: Modern Languages (1968)	45p
48. Maiden Erlegh Secondary School (1973)	80p
49. Abraham Moss Centre (1973)	80p

OTHER EDUCATIONAL BUILDINGS

18. Schools in the USA: A Report (1961)	75p
20. Youth Service Buildings: General Mixed Clubs (1961)	20p
27. Boarding Schools for Maladjusted Children (1965)	25p
29. Harris College, Preston (1966)	70p

TECHNICAL SUBJECTS

4. Cost Study (3rd edition (1972))	£1.13
7. Fire and the Design of Schools (1975)	£2.50
9. Colour in School Buildings (4th edition (1969))	57½p
19. The Story of CLASP (1961)	25p
21. Remodelling Old Schools (1963)	50p
28. Playing Fields and Hard Surface Areas (1966)	68p
38. School Furniture Dimensions: Standing and Reaching (1967)	65p
42. The Co-ordination of Components for Educational Building (1968)	29p
44. Furniture and Equipment Dimensions: Further and Higher Education, 18 to 25 Age Group (1970)	30p
45. CLASP/JDP: the Development of a Building System for Higher Education (1970)	75p
46. British School Population Dimensional Survey (1971)	65p
50. Furniture and Equipment Working Heights and Zones for Practical Activities (1973)	45p
51. Acoustics in Educational Buildings (1975)	£2.00
52. School Furniture (1976)	£1.20
54. The Consortia (1976)	75p
55. Energy Conservation in Educational Buildings (1977)	£1.30

Building Bulletins are published by Her Majesty's Stationery Office. (Prices do not include postage.)

Publications (continued)

Design Notes

1. Building for Nursery Education (1968)
2. Henry Fanshawe School, Dronfield, Derbyshire (1969)
3. Demonstration Rig: Component Fixing Conventions (1969)
4. A visit to some Swedish Schools (1967) (Out of Print)
5. The School and the Community (1970)
6. Sedgefield School, Durham (1970)
7. USA Visit (1970)
8. Polytechnics: Planning for Development (1972)
9. Designing for Further Education (1973)
10. Designing for the Severely Handicapped (1972)
11. Chaucer Infant and Nursery School, Ilkeston, Derbyshire (1973)
12. Space Utilization in Universities and Polytechnics (1974)
14. School and Community-2 (1976)
15. Crewe Central Area Development (1977)
16. Energy Conservation in two Oxfordshire Schools (1978)

Design Notes are available free of charge from the Publications Despatch Centre, Department of Education and Science, Honeypot Lane, Canons Park, Stanmore, Middlesex.

Architects and Building Papers

Paper No 1 Abraham Moss Centre, Manchester, a progress report (1978)

Paper No 2 The Clayton Green District Centre (1978)

A & B Papers are available free of charge from Architects and Building Branch, Department of Education and Science, Elizabeth House, York Road, London SE1 7PH.

Welsh Education Office Publications

DESIGN STUDIES

1. Small Rural Primary Schools in Wales (1975)
2. Ysgol y Dderi: An Area School in Dyfed (1976)

Design Studies are available free of charge from:

The Welsh Office Education Department, Government Buildings, Ty Glas, Llanishen, Cardiff.

The Welsh Office Education Department, Regent House, Regent Street, Wrexham, Clwyd.

Laboratories Investigation Unit Publications

Paper No 1 An Approach to Laboratory Building: A Paper for Discussion (1969)

Paper No 2 Deep or Shallow Building: A comparison of Costs in Use (1970)

Paper No 3 Growth and Change in Laboratory Activity (1971)

Paper No 4 The Economics of Adaptability (1971)

Paper No 5 Conversions of Buildings for Science and Technology (1971)

Paper No 6 Adaptable furniture and services for Education and Science (1972)

Paper No 7 Adaptable Laboratories: Practical Observations on Design and Installation (1974)

Paper No 8 The Conversion of Buildings for Science and Technology (1977)

Paper No 9 The Charles Darwin Building. £4.00 Bristol Polytechnic (1977)

Paper No 10 Research Laboratories: Design for Flexibility (1977)

LIU Publications (except Paper No 9) are available free of charge from the Laboratories Investigation Unit, Department of Education and Science, Elizabeth House, York Road, London SE1 7PH.

LIU Paper No 9 is obtainable from Her Majesty's Stationery Office. (Price does not include postage.)

Other Publications relating to Educational Buildings

A Study of School Building (1977)   £5.50 obtainable from Her Majesty's Stationery Office.